A WORKBOOK OF

LITERACY BASED SELECTED ACTIVITIES TO ACCOMPANY

CHOSEN VESSELS

THE UNITING OF AMERICA'S PROMISES BEFORE
THE SEMIQUINCENTENNIAL

A WORKBOOK OF

LITERACY BASED SELECTED ACTIVITIES TO ACCOMPANY

CHOSEN VESSELS

THE UNITING OF AMERICA'S PROMISES BEFORE THE SEMIQUINCENTENNIAL

Elizabeth Grady Branch, EdD

PROJECT STAND-UP BOOK PUBLISHING

Fort Worth, Texas

A WORKBOOK OF
SELECTED LITERACY-BASED ACTIVITIES TO ACCOMPANY
CHOSEN VESSELS
THE UNITING OF AMERICA'S PROMISES BEFORE
THE SEMIQUINCENTENNIAL
Published by
Project Stand-Up Book Publishing
Email: theprojectstandup@gmail.com

Elizabeth Grady Branch, EdD, Publisher & Editorial Director
Jokwon Bagby, MS, Contributing Editor
Jamese Michelle Branch, BA, Contributing Editor

Yvonne Rose, Editor
QualityPress.info, Production Coordinator

CONTENTS

INTRODUCTION

Smart Scholars are determined to increase their literacy skills. The Workbook of Selected Activities provides one way to improve your college readiness vocabulary. Over the next few weeks, you will gain or review skills that you can use every day for the rest of your life!

No matter what position or educational level you are on presently, or where you intend to go later in life, literacy is extremely important. Improving these skills and increasing your vocabulary is never a waste of time. You will use your vocabulary in speaking, listening, reading, writing, spelling, and processing critical thinking skills wherever you are. It is a lifetime investment and a reward. Completing these exercises will help you to find comfortable ways to begin work toward the accomplishment of this task.

So, Scholars, enjoy these activities as you review some of what you have read and discussed and add these new skills to your college readiness skills set.

In addition to the important tidbits of historical information included here, we have used some of the vocabulary from the contents of "CHOSEN VESSELS" in these activities.

Have fun while you are learning!

PART ONE

SELECTED WORKBOOK ACTIVITIES
LESSONS 1-18

LESSON 1 - HOMONYMS/HOMOPHONES

Scholars may already know how to spell and use these homonyms. The mastery of knowing these and others is an important skill needed for VOCABULARY DEVELOPMENT and WRITTEN communications. These words are often confusing, so study them carefully. Here are 20 commonly confused HOMOPHONES. These are words that sound the same, but they are spelled differently. An example is MAID and MADE. These words have different meanings. After you have read this list, add five more sets on the lines below. Include a brief meaning.

1. Bare is an adjective. It describes being uncovered.
2. Bear is a noun that refers to a large, carnivorous animal.
3. Capital is a noun that refers to a city or town that serves as the official seat of government.
4. Capital is a command of a letter of the alphabet that is written or printed in its large form (Aa, Bb, Cc).
5. Capitol is a noun that refers to a building in which a legislative assembly meets.
6. Complement is a noun that refers to something that completes or brings to perfection.
7. Compliment is a noun that refers to an expression of praise or admiration.
8. Council is a noun that refers to a group of people who are elected or chosen to make decisions or give advice.
9. Counsel is a noun that refers to advice or guidance given by a lawyer or other professional.
10. Desert is a noun. It is a dry, barren area of land.
11. It may be a verb that means to abandon or leave.
12. Dessert is a noun that refers to a sweet course served at the end of a meal.
13. Fair is an adjective. Sometimes it means just or reasonable.
14. Fare is a noun that refers to the money paid for a journey in a vehicle.
15. Wave is a verb that means to make a motion with your hand.
16. Waive is to give up claim to.
17. Hear is a verb. It means to perceive or understand with the ear the sound made by someone or something.
18. Here is an adverb that means in, at, or to this place or position.
19. its/it's: Its is a possessive pronoun. It means belonging to or associated with a thing previously mentioned or easily identified.
20. It's is a contraction of it is or it has.

1	/
2	/
3	/
4	/
5	/

Here are 10 homonyms, homographs, and homophones: Remember, these are words that are not spelled the same, but they sound the same. They do not mean the same. This is especially important in reading comprehension and listening skill development. Add five more to the list in the spaces provided below. Add a brief meaning.

1. **lead/led**: Lead is a verb. It means to guide or direct. Led is the past tense of lead.

2. **loose/lose**: Loose is an adjective that means not firmly or tightly fixed in place. Lose is a verb that means to be deprived of or cease to have or retain.

3. **principal/principle**: Principal is a noun that refers to the person with the highest authority or position in an organization. Principle is a noun that refers to a fundamental truth, proposition, foundation of belief, or behavior.

4. **quiet/quite**: Quiet is an adjective that means making little or no noise. Quite is an adverb that means to the utmost or completely.

5. **stationary/stationery**: Stationary is an adjective that means not moving or still. Stationery is a noun that refers to writing paper, especially with matching envelopes.

6. **than/then**: Than is a conjunction used in comparisons. Then is an adverb that means at that time or next in order of time.

7. **their/there/they're**: Their is a pronoun that means belonging to or associated with people or things previously mentioned or easily identified. There is an adverb that means in, at, or to that place or position. They're is a contraction of they are.

8. **to/too/two**: To is a preposition that expresses motion or direction toward a point, person, place, or thing. Too is an adverb that means also or in addition. Two is a number.

9. **waist/waste**: Waist is a noun that refers to the part of the human body below the ribs and above the hips. Waste is a noun that refers to material that is not wanted or needed or of no purpose.

10. **whose/who's**: Whose is a possessive pronoun that means belonging to or associated with which person. Who's is a contraction of who is or who has.

1 __________________	/ __________________
2 __________________	/ __________________
3 __________________	/ __________________
4 __________________	/ __________________
5 __________________	/ __________________

Here are 10 HOMOGRAPHS. Be prepared to USE YOUR DRAWING SKILLS in this activity. These are words that are spelled the same way. They are spelled one way   They sound one way. BUT they have different meanings in different situations. This is especially important to know in writing and reading comprehension skill development. We will teach you the lessons through these repetitions or rewriting of the correct word (using cursive script). Then you CHOOSE ANY FIVE from this list to demonstrate (in picture form) your understanding of their meanings. Use the spaces provided for this activity on the next page in lesson 4. Be prepared to explain your drawings.

1. **Bow**: is a word for a weapon for shooting arrows. A ____can be a knot tied with two loops and two loose ends.
2. **Game:** is the word for a sport or activity. ______ can be an animal or fowl that is hunted.
3. **Cell**: is a small room. A _____ can be a basic unit of life.
4. **Love**: is a tennis score or _____ can be a feeling or emotion.
5. **Match**: is a short, thin piece of wood used to start a fire. A _____ can be a game or a competition.
6. **Space**: is an area or region beyond the earth's atmosphere or a _______ is an area set apart.
7. **Unit**: is a portion of a school course or a ______ can be a single part of a whole.
8. **Stick:** is a piece of wood or ______ is an informal word for defraud.
9. **Enough:** is a sufficient amount or _______ means tolerable.
10. **Bend:** is a curve in the road or to ______ is to turn the body in a certain direction.
11. **Flag:** is an alert or warning or a ______ is a piece of cloth with a special design or symbol.
12. **Fly:** is a word meaning for an airplane trip or a _____ is a winged insect.
13. **School:** is a special building or _______ is a slang term for learning informally.
14. **Dope:** is a term used in the Civil Rights era to describe an illegal drug or ______ is an anachronistic and unacceptable term (shown in some dictionaries) for "a 'stupid' person."
15. **Period:** is a tool used to end a sentence or a ____ is a length of time.

 # Right____ X 10 = ______ Score

DRAW FIVE PICTURES ON THE NEXT PAGE (LESSON 4) TO DEMONSTRATE YOUR UNDERSTANDING OF THESE HOMOGRAPHS.

LESSON 4 - HOMONYMS/HOMOGRAPHS/ DRAWINGS

Here are five boxes for a word from lesson 3 to be entered each time. (Use another paper if you would like). CHOOSE ANY FIVE words from the list above. Be prepared to USE YOUR BEST DRAWING SKILLS in this activity! (However, none will count against you). Draw two (2) images representing the one (1) word chosen in each box. Proudly, share with the leader and others around you. Be prepared to explain your drawings. (DRAWINGS WILL VARY)

1

2

3

4

5

LESSON 5 - SYNONYMS, SPELLING, HANDWRITING

Here are 10 SYNONYMS. These are words that are not spelled the same. They do not sound the same. BUT they mean the same. This is especially important in reading comprehension and listening skill development. They help with writing skills because you do not need to be redundant or use the same words over and over in essays. Match their meanings of sameness to you. Then add your own ten sets of words using this pattern. You may use the dictionary.

1. diversity _______   a. useful

2. bigotry _______   b. accolades

3. wisdom _______   c. helpless

4. futile _______   d. sagacity

5. tributes _______   e. plural

6. stipulated _______   f. believe

7. viable _______   g. racism

8. compel _______   h. free

9. assume _______   i. named

10. emancipate _______   j. drive

Add 10 new synonyms and a match here in your best handwriting.

1. _______________________   _______________

2. _______________________   _______________

3. _______________________   _______________

4. _______________________   _______________

5. _______________________   _______________

6. _______________________   _______________

7. _______________________   _______________

8. _______________________   _______________

9. _______________________   _______________

10. _______________________   _______________

 # Right_____ X 10 = _______ Score

Here are 10 ANTONYMS: These are words that DO NOT spell the same. They DO NOT sound the same. AND, they are directly OPPOSITES in meanings from each other. This is especially important in vocabulary, reading comprehension, and listening skill development. First, we will teach you. Then you add five more sets to the list in the spaces provided to show us you understand.

Example: Integration   Segregation

1. Peace   Conflict
2. Strong   Weak
3. Abroad   Local
4. Restrained   Boundary
5. Jubilant   Sad
6. Equitable   Unfair
7. Unity   Division
8. Order   Chaos
9. Sagacity   Ignorance
10. Poverty   Wealth

1 _____________________________ / _____________________________
2 _____________________________ / _____________________________
3 _____________________________ / _____________________________
4 _____________________________ / _____________________________
5 _____________________________ / _____________________________

Match these antonyms: Remember they are opposites in meaning.

1. Peace ___   a. Abroad
2. Strong ___   b. Jubilant
3. Local ___   c. Divided
4. Restrained ___   d. Unbound
5. Sad ___   e. Weak
6. Equitable ___   f. Unfair
7. Unity___   g. Division
8. Chaos ___   h. Wealth
9. Sagacity___   i. Ignorance
10. Poverty ___   j. Conflict

 # Right_____ X 10 = _______ Score

Here are 10 ANTONYMS: These are words that DO NOT spell the same. They DO NOT sound the same. AND, they are directly opposite in meaning from each other. This is especially important in reading comprehension and listening skill development. First, we will teach you. Then you add five more sets to the list in the spaces provided to show us you understand.

1. Amicable   Unfriendly
2. Introvert   Outgoing
3. Weak   Powerful
4. Tenacity   loose
5. Inform   Withhold
6. Certain   Inevitable
7. Purposeful   Intentional
8. Divide   Separate
9. Contribute   Add
10. Unafraid   Valor

Now write five additional pairs of ANTONYMS.

1 ______________________ / ______________________
2 ______________________ / ______________________
3 ______________________ / ______________________
4 ______________________ / ______________________
5 ______________________ / ______________________

Match these ANTONYMS using the correct numbers:

1. Introvert   ___ intentional
2. Weak   ___ outgoing
3. Amicable   ___ valor
4. Unafraid   ___ hold
5. Certain   ___ powerful
6. Tenacity   ___ inevitable
7. Inform   ___ separate
8. divide   ___ unfriendly
9. contribute   ___ tell
10. purposeful   ___ add

 # Right______ X 10 = ________ Score

CHALLENGE YOUR FRIENDS! Here is a list of 15 words that are not all spelled correctly. One is correct on each line. Circle the correct one. This is especially important in writing, spelling, reading comprehension, and other literacy skill developments. Add five more *new and difficult* words from the lessons in CHOSEN VESSELS (or any American history lessons) in the spaces provided. Discuss them with your leader.

1.	American	Amercan	Americin	Americain
2.	Patreot	Patriot	Patriok	Patroit
3.	Unittedd	Uniteed	United	Unnnitted
4.	Civil	Civel	Civvel	Civiel
5.	Constiituion	Cunstition	Constitution	Constiution
6.	Ancesstors	Ancestors	Anacestos	Anscetors
7.	Continent	Countint	Conttinet	Cuntinnent
8.	Plege	pleadge	Pledge	Pleagge
9.	Histry	Histroy	History	Histrory
10.	Enforcement	Enforcment	Enforment	Enforsement
11.	Weallth	Waleth	Wealeth	Wealth
12.	Faith	Fiath	Fathe	Faetjh
13.	Allegiance	Alegiance	Aledgiance	Alligiyunce
14.	Centruy	Cintry	Century	Cenntury
15.	Idigenous	Indegous	Indigenous	Idianeous

```
1 _______________________________ / ___________________________________
2 _______________________________ / ___________________________________
3 _______________________________ / ___________________________________
4 _______________________________ / ___________________________________
5 _______________________________ / ___________________________________
```

 # Right_____ X 5 = _______ Score

(ANSWERS WILL VARY)

DRAWINGS OF AMERICAN SYMBOLS. Here are 5 boxes for your special drawings. We will intentionally revisit patriotic symbols that every young American Scholar should be familiar with leading up to the Semiquincentennial. You may use another paper if your leader agrees. Here are the tasks to perform.

1. **Outline Our U.S. Map as it is Shown on the North American Continent.**

2. **Construct Your Own Drawing of The Us Flag.** (Use red, white, and blue colors. Show the correct # of stars, and stripes).

3. **Write the Pledge of Allegiance in your best cursive handwriting.**

4. **Draw the medals identifying the 6 Branches of the armed military services. Label them. Indicate any member of your family (or friend) who served.**

5. **Draw the US Seal with the phrase E Pluribus Unum (out of many, one) included.**

Here are 20 words that are spelled correctly. Write the number of parts (or syllables) you hear in each one. This is especially important in writing, spelling, phonics, speaking, and reading comprehension skill development. Add five more to the list in the spaces provided. Discuss them with your leader(s) or classmates.

1. Hope   _______
2. Rights   _______
3. Citizen   _______
4. Revolution   _______
5. Emancipation   _______
6. Slavery   _______
7. Brutality   _______
8. Nation   _______
9. United States   _______   _____
10. Semiquincentennial   _______
11. Racism   _______
12. Liberty   _______
13. Indigenous   _______
14. Christianity   _______
15. American   _______
16. Reconstruction   _______
17. E Pluribus unum   _______
18. Massacres   _______
19. Abolitionist   _______
20. Supremacy   _______

BONUS

21. Inequality   _______
22. Auctions   _______

1 _______________	/	_______________
2 _______________	/	_______________
3 _______________	/	_______________
4 _______________	/	_______________
5 _______________	/	_______________

 # Right_______ **X 5 =** _______ **Score**

Here are 20 WORDS THAT your leader will choose from the previous lesson for you to write and spell. Your leader will choose another student to call them out. Choose a partner to make sure you both can spell the words correctly. Write them as best you can in Column A. WORK TOGETHER, BUT EACH OF YOU SHOULD HAVE YOUR OWN LIST on your own paper. Your leader will allow you to check your work orally. Write the words you did not spell correctly in Column B. This lesson is especially important in spelling, writing, listening, reading comprehension, and social skill development. All lessons are good at teaching you to follow directions. Add five more to share in a spelling match with your friends. Discuss them with your leader.

COLUMN A

1. ___________________________
2. ___________________________
3. ___________________________
4. ___________________________
5. ___________________________
6. ___________________________
7. ___________________________
8. ___________________________
9. ___________________________
10. ___________________________
11. ___________________________
12. ___________________________
13. ___________________________
14. ___________________________
15. ___________________________
16. ___________________________
17. ___________________________
18. ___________________________
19. ___________________________
20. ___________________________

COLUMN B

1. ___________________________
2. ___________________________
3. ___________________________
4. ___________________________
5. ___________________________
6. ___________________________
7. ___________________________
8. ___________________________
9. ___________________________
10 ___________________________
11. ___________________________
12. ___________________________
14. ___________________________
15. ___________________________
16. ___________________________
17. ___________________________
17. ___________________________
18. ___________________________
19. ___________________________
20. ___________________________

Share These with Your Class.

1 ___________________________
2 ___________________________
3 ___________________________
4 ___________________________
5 ___________________________

Right_____ X 5 = _______ Score

Arrange these documents in chronological order of preparedness for the Semiquincentennial. Write a number from 1- 9 to show their order of occurrences in our history. (Ask your leader if you might review your lesson _____ in your "CHOSEN VESSELS" book. The chapter will help you to recall this information and the order of occurrences. Write a brief explanation for how it helped Americans in our diverse culture.

Order of Issuance   Designed to Help Americans

_Year: ________________ **The United States = Constitution:** ____________________________

____

_Year:________________ **The Emancipation:** ____

____

_Year:________________ **The 14th Amendment:** ______________________________________

____

_Year:________________ **The 13th Amendment:** ______________________________________

____

_Year:________________ **The 15th Amendment:** ______________________________________

____

_Year: ________________ **The Civil Rights Act of 1964:** _________________________________

____

_Year:________________ **Executive order 1981:** _____________________________________

____

_Year________________ **The Voting Rights Act of 1965:** _______________________________

____

_Year_________________ **The Civil Rights Act of 1866:** _______________________________

____

 # Right_____ X 10 = _______ Score

LESSON 13 - READING COMPREHENSION, SUPPORTING DETAILS, WRITING, SEQUENCE

Arrange these eras of movement leading up to the Semiquincentennial. Write a number from 1- 6 to show their level of chronological order. Write a brief explanation for how you think each helped Americans in our diverse culture to become more united. Be prepared to defend your choices.

1______________________ **Jim Crow** ____

____

____

2______________________ **Reconstruction** ____

____

____

3______________________ **Slavery** ____

____

____

4______________________ **Black Lives Matte**_______________________________________

____

____

5______________________ **Civil Rights Movement** __________________________________

____

____

BONUS

6______________________ **Semiquincentennial** _____________________________________

____

____

 # Right_____ X 20 = _______ Score

These statements are true or false. Write T or F on the lines provided after the number. Write comments on the lines provided for discussion purposes. These lessons help with memorization, reading comprehension, and critical thinking skills.

1. _______White Americans helped organize the National Association for the Advancement of Colored People (NAACP).
Comments: ____

2. _______African Americans or Black-skinned people were living in this country before Columbus "discovered" it as America.
Comments: ____

3. _______The "Lift Every Voice and Sing" lyrics are older than the "Star-Spangled Banner" lyrics.
Comments: ____

4. _______ Many White American slave owners were the first recipients of reparations for having to free their slaves in 1865.
Comments: ____

5. _______ Blacks and Indians owned slaves and fought against the abolition or ending of this evil and brutal system in America.
Comments: ____

6. _______The 19th Amendment extended the right to vote to White women only in 1920. It did not extend this "equal right" to vote to Black Women at that time.
Comments: ____

7. _______Only White Americans fought in the American military branches of the United States of America.
Comments: ____

8. _______Few laws against killings, lynching, and other forms of brutality protected Black Americans many years after slavery. No one was ever held accountable for the Leesburg Stockade Scandal in Georgia.
Comments: ____

9. _______ Nat Turner's Rebellion and John Browns's Raid at Harper's Ferry were a success because they were proponents of violence.

10. _______All major fights, insurrections, and raids against slavery, civil rights, Jim Crow, and other acts of disagreement and violence were done by Black Americans.

BONUS

11. _______ America's diversity is increasing by the minute.

 # Right_____ X 10 = _______ Score

Scholars will acquire and extend their academic vocabulary in order to be successful in college. Here are 10 sample words on that level. Read the list and their meanings. Then place the correct word in the sentences below. This helps your literacy skills in all areas. It helps you to speak, listen, read, and know what to expect at a college level.

1. **Discredit:** put to shame; disgrace.
2. **Emulate:** try to equal or imitate.
3. **Integrity:** morally upright, honesty, sincerity
4. **Opponents:** opposite sides
5. **Enhance:** add to something; give more
6. **Inevitable:** bound to happen
7. **Resilient:** bounce back after loss, return
8. **Exasperated:** irritated greatly, infuriated, made very angry
9. **Exemplary:** commendable, exceptional
10. **Inconsequential:** Trivial, doesn't matter, not leading to consequences

Place these words in these sentences. Skip the ones that you do not know and come back to them.

1. Our favorite, smart, and ______________ candidate was behind as the polls were drawing to a close.

2. Of course, we were frustrated, ______________, and disappointed in the voters' turnout and choice.

3. The ______________, or our competition, had an outstanding campaign leader.

4. The weather did not help improve or ______________ our chances and possibilities either.

5. We will ______________ and imitate some of their speeches and strategies during the next election.

6. We cannot ______________ their efforts by accusing them of cheating.

7. Losing a tough race like this is not ______________, and the evaluations will be rigorous.

8. However, if we keep working this hard, it is ______________ that our candidate will win.

9. Our candidate shows ______________ on and off the campaign trail.

10. He is ______________ and will return stronger than ever for the next campaign.

 # Right______ X 10 = ______ Score

Match these college-level readiness words and their meanings. You may use a dictionary. Then write a sentence in the spaces below using the word. This will help to increase your college-level readiness vocabulary. It helps to familiarize you with the many literacy tools available in your personal dictionary and hand-held devices. Discuss any concerns.

Part A: Vocabulary

1. Sagacity _____
2. Tenacious _____
3. Transient _____
4. Vindicate _____
5. Tactful _____
6. Wary _____
7. Subtle _____
8. Submissive _____
9. Substantiate _____
10. Extrovert _____

Part B: Meanings

a. meek and humble
b. watchful, alert
c. verify, confirm,
d. elusive, sly
e. not stable, moving, in motion
f. wisdom, knowing, wise
g. polite, diplomatic
h. hangs on, unmovable
i. clear from blame or wrongdoings
j. outgoing

Choose any 5 new words and write five sentences here. (ANSWERS WILL VARY)

1. ____
   ____

2. ____
   ____

3. ____
   ____

4. ____
   ____

5. ____
   ____

 # Right_____ X 10 = _______ Score

LESSON 17 - READING FOR UNDERSTANDING

Some amazing and amusing historical data notes from the contents of "CHOSEN VESSELS" are included here. Understanding what you read is a lifetime investment. Place the proper words (synonyms, antonyms, etc.) in the sentences to help them make sense to you.

1. The __________ of the gold broke the axle on the wagon's back wheels.
    a. Sneak **b.** steal **c.** wait **d.** weight **e.** team

2. Our earliest ancestors first church services, praise and __________ were not held in sanctuaries. They were held in isolated, secretive spots called "hush harbors".
    a. Base **b.** steps **c.** towns **d.** worship **e.** dogs

3. If you are queried, or you are __________ about the number of soap bubbles that are in a bar of soap, would you be concerned about the motive?
    a. answered **b.** questioned **c.** written **d.** told **e.** kept

4. An American history course to show the uniting of our states should be __________ for every US citizen in our diverse society.
    a. vaccine **b.** unity **c.** mandatory **d.** hidden **e.** used

5. At least __________ Indigenous tribes were represented during the formation of the US Constitution council meetings.
    a. further **b.** colony **c.** eight **d.** better **e.** ate

6. You do not have to drive __________ to vote in most elections.
    a. pen **b.** far **c.** for **d.** little **e.** book

7. If the Constitution is filled with racism and __________ , it cannot serve a diverse population.
    a. bigotry **b.** single **c.** outgoing **d.** light **e.** unused

8. Cotton, corn, and sugar cane were hot __________ in making America a wealthy nation.
    a. Homes **b.** roads **c.** commodities **d.** rode **e.** cars

9. Some World War II ammunition was made from __________ plastics and other materials.
    a. Recycled **b.** powerless **c.** motion **d.** weather **e.** crops

10. If it transpires before the Semiquincentennial, it will __________ before 2026.
    a. Win **b.** vote **c.** false **d.** law **e.** happen

 # Right______ X 10 = _______ Score

Scholars do not fear using words that are not a part of their everyday conversations. They can break them down into smaller parts to gain meaning and the proper way of pronouncing them, phonetically. With the aid of your English dictionary's pronunciation symbols, you can unlock the key to speaking or saying any word. LEARN TO USE THE SYMBOLS KEY! Practice these 10 words and break them into each part you hear. Practice reading and saying these new vocabulary words. Learn to spell these words without looking at them. Use your dictionary if you are unsure of the meaning.

FOR PRACTICE IN KNOWING HOW TO MAKE THE CORRECT PRONUNCIATIONS WHEN ENCOUNTERING BIG WORDS IN THE FUTURE, COPY EVERY MARK OR SYMBOL USED IN YOUR PRONUNCIATION KEY FOR EACH WORD LISTED. *(DICTIONARY KEYS WILL VARY)*

1. Monolithic
2. Humongous
3. Divisiveness
4. Anachronistic
5. Sagacity
6. Constitution
7. Bibliotherapy
8. Semiquincentennial
9. Capitalism
10. E Pluribus unum

a. _______ _____ _____ _____
b. _____ _____ _____
c. _____ _____ _____ _____
d. _____ _____ _____ _____ ____
e. _____ _____ _____ _____
f. _____ _____ _____ _____
g. ____ ____ ____ ____ ____ _____
h. ____ ____ _____ _____ ____ ____
i. ____ ____ ____ ____ ____
j. _____ _____ ____ ____ ____ ___

MATCH THESE MEANINGS. DRAW LINES FROM THE NUMBERS TO THEIR MEANINGS. USE YOUR DICTIONARY FOR MORE UNDERSTANDING.

11. Monolithic
12. Humongous
13. Divisiveness
14. Anachronistic
15. Sagacity
16. Constitution
17. Bibliotherapy
18. Semiquincentennial
19. Capitalism
20. E Pluribus unum

a. huge, gigantic, very large
b. old-fashioned, out-of-date
c. basic beliefs, rights, laws established
d. an economic system
e. a celebratory period for 250 years
f. using books to treat mental stress
g. out of many, one
h. separate, individualistic, segregate
i. wisdom, knowledge, wise
j. one-sided view, opinionated

 # Right_____ X 5 = _______ Score

PART TWO

HISTORY EXERCISES
"CHOSEN VESSELS: UNITING OF THE STATES OF AMERICA BEFORE THE SEMIQUINCENTENNIAL"

In the book, "Chosen Vessels: Uniting of the States of America Before the Semiquincentennial," we have selected a few American Citizens who were Activists during the Jim Crow and Civil Rights eras to name here. Further discussion will help preserve the memories of those as well as other Heroes and Sheroes. In continuing to research their contributions, many great American names, Black and White (as well as other people of color), will emerge.

These twelve chosen White American legacies fought fearlessly and with valor against hate. They were fighting for America's idea of freedom and liberty for all American citizens. Their names and contributions dedicated to making America great for a diverse society will live on through other Americans like you! Because of their sacrifices, all Americans, as well as our ancestors can proudly celebrate and commemorate our Semiquincentennial.

Imagine what our Semiquincentennial might have looked like without their efforts, as well as some of their friends!

Here, I have a recap of the vignettes included in "Chosen Vessels" so you can continue with further research and discussions.

Enjoy these lessons!

1. **Pastor James Reeb**: Civil Rights Activist and Minister who answered King's call for help. He was beaten by a trio of white men for helping blacks to achieve voting rights.

I believe **Pastor James Reeb** is a hero. Share your thoughts with me …

____

____

____

____

____

____

____

2. **Viola Liuzzo**: American Civil Rights Activist; NAACP member and Civil Rights Volunteer. She was murdered by the KKK while assisting in Black voter's rights.

I believe **Viola Liuzzo** is a shero. Share your thoughts with me …

____

____

____

____

____

____

____

____

3. **Danny Lyons:** Student Civil Rights Activist; and SNCC Photographer. He broke the Leesburg Stockade unforgettable scandal against the young Black American girls in Georgia.

I believe **Danny Lyons** is a hero. Share your thoughts with me …

____

____

____

____

____

____

____

____

____

____

4. **Claibourne Paul Ellis**: Ex -KKK, Exalted Grand Cyclops who left the Klan and became a Civil Rights Activist; Trade Union Organizer. He lost many friends, but he gained some, too.

I believe **Claibourne Paul Ellis** is a hero. Share your thoughts with me …

____

____

____

____

____

____

____

____

____

5. **Juliette H. Morgan**: wealthy; Civil Rights Activist; librarian, educator; may have committed suicide from community pressures. She was later recognized for efforts in Civil Rights struggles.

I believe **Juliette H. Morgan** is a shero. Share your thoughts with me …

____

____

____

____

____

____

____

____

6. **Michael Schwerner**: White American Civil Rights activist; CORE volunteer. He was murdered in Mississippi at the hands of other whites for helping Blacks gain their equal rights in America.

I believe **Michael Schwerner** is a hero. Share your thoughts with me …

____

____

____

____

____

____

____

____

7. **Andrew Goodman**: White Civil Rights activist, CORE volunteer and member. He was killed by the KKK in Mississippi in 1964 while assisting Blacks in their struggle for equality in America.

I believe **Andrew Goodman** is a hero. Share your thoughts with me …

____

____

____

____

____

____

____

____

____

8. **Joseph I Reiff**: Minister/Author/Signer; Author: "Born of Conviction; White Methodist and Mississippi's Closed Society." He hoped to lead the way to better relations among clergy, congregations, and Americans who supported nonviolent movement for equal rights.

I believe **Joseph I Reiff** is a hero. Share your thoughts with me …

____

____

____

____

____

____

____

____

9. **Bruce Klunder**: White American Civil Rights Activist and CORE member. He was accidentally run over while demonstrating against the unfair treatment of Black Americans and their equal rights.

I believe **Bruce Klunder** is a hero. Share your thoughts with me …

____

____

____

____

____

____

____

____

____

____

10. **James Peck:** White American Civil Rights activist and CORE Freedom Rider. He was promoted peaceful nonviolent demonstrations, brutally beaten many times.

I believe **James Peck** is a hero. Share your thoughts with me …

____

____

____

____

____

____

____

____

____

____

11. **William L Moore**: CORE Volunteer and U.S. Postman was shot during a march against segregation. He was murdered outside of Attalla, Alabama, where he intended to deliver a letter to Governor Ross Barnett, supporting civil rights.

I believe **William L Moore** is a hero. Share your thoughts with me …

____

____

____

____

____

____

____

____

12. **Jonathan M. Daniels:** Episcopal seminarian and civil rights activist. In 1965, he was killed by a part-time special county deputy, while saving the life of a young Black civil rights activist. He. shared a jail cell with Stokley Carmichael and other Civil Rights advocates.

I believe **Jonathan M. Daniels** is a hero. Share your thoughts with me …

____

____

____

____

____

____

____

____

LESSON 20 - GENERATING CONVERSATION WITH ELDERLY FAMILY MEMBERS AND FRIENDS

There are reasons to try to initiate conversations between the elderly and young people. The major reasons are to combat ageism, and racism, gain wisdom and knowledge, and learn more about our history. History helps rid America of hate when the truth is revealed. Elderly people have lived through many historical events. In some instances, we are the history! We can provide a unique perspective, accolades, warnings, and words of advice for our listeners. We can share personal experiences and stories that can remove stereotypes about aging and provide valuable input into life, work, and relationships. Conversing can help younger people value the elderly as worthy Americans rather than just a monolithic group. This lesson will offer valuable conversation starters for discussions with elders.

A. SHARE THIS PROJECT'S CONTENT WITH ANYONE IN YOUR FAMILY, CHURCH, or COMMUNITY CIRCLE.

B. GET UP CLOSE AND PERSONAL INFORMATION ABOUT YOUR OWN FAMILY'S HISTORY, NOW! LATER YOU WILL BE GLAD YOU DID. TALK TO YOUR "GRANDS'! ONCE YOU START, IT IS HARD TO STOP. THEY HAVE AMAZING STORIES TO SHARE.

C. OBITUARIES CONTAIN LOTS OF HELPFUL FAMILY HISTORY AND INFORMATION FOR AFRICAN AMERICAN FAMILIES. KEEP UP WITH THEM. STORE THEM IN YOUR BIBLE AREA OR WITH OTHER KEEPSAKES.

D. ANCESTRY.COM AND SIMILAR ORGANIZATIONS ARE HELPFUL.

ACTIVITY:

RANK in order YOUR idea of which topic listed below1-8, plus your 2, that would be of the most interest to you as a young scholar engaged in a conversation with an elder---70-year-olds (septuagenarian), 80-year-olds (octogenarian), 90-year-olds (nonagenarian), or even a 100-years-old (centenarian).

____

____

____

____

____

TOPICS OF CONVERSATION WITH ELDERS:
RANK IN ORDER OF IMPORTANCE WITH 1 BEING THE MOST IDEAL.

1. What do you think about life and world changes over these 250 years? _________
    ____
    ____

2. Despite adversities, tell me about some of your most cherished memories from your
    childhood. ____
    ____
    ____

3. Share with me your current hobbies and interests now compared to your childhood.
    ____
    ____

4. In looking back over your wonderful years, what have been the most important things
    you have learned in life? ____
    ____
    ____

5. Let's talk about a good life…what is that like to you? ________________________
    ____
    ____

6. Were times ever so hard in school you just did not think you would make it another day?
    ____
    ____

7. What advice would you give me to overcome feelings of inferiority?
    ____
    ____

8. If you could do everything all over again, which two or three things would you
    readily repeat? ____
    ____
    ____

ADD TWO OF YOUR OWN DISCUSSION TOPICS HERE:

____

____

____

____

PART THREE

ANSWER KEYS FOR LESSONS 1-18

LESSON 3 - HOMONYMS/HOMOGRAPHS, SPELLING, WRITING, DRAWINGS

Here are 10 HOMOGRAPHS. Be prepared to USE YOUR DRAWING SKILLS in this activity. These are words that are spelled the same way. They are spelled one way   They sound one way. BUT they have different meanings in different situations. This is especially important to know in writing and reading comprehension skill development. We will teach you the lessons through these repetitions or rewriting of the correct word (using cursive). Then you CHOOSE ANY FIVE from this list to demonstrate (in picture form) your understanding of their meanings. Use the spaces provided for this activity on the next page in lesson 4. Be prepared to explain your drawings.

1. **Bow**: is a word for a weapon for shooting arrows. A *bow* can be a knot tied with two loops and two loose ends.

2. **Game:** is a word for a sport or activity. *Game* can be an animal or fowl that is hunted.

3. **Cell**: is a small room. A *cell* can be a basic unit of life.

4. **Love**: is a tennis score or *love* can be a feeling or emotion.

5. **Match**: is a short, thin piece of wood used to start a fire. A *match* can be a game or a competition.

6. **Space**: is an area or region beyond the earth's atmosphere or a *space* is an area set apart.

7. **Unit**: is a portion of a school course or a *unit* can be a single part of a whole.

8. **Stick:** is a piece of wood or *stick* is an informal word for defraud.

9. **Enough:** is a sufficient amount or *enough* means tolerable.

10. **Bend**: is a curve in the road or to *bend* is to turn the body in a certain direction.

11. **Flag:** is an alert or warning or a *flag* is a piece of cloth with a special design or symbol.

12. **Fly:** is a word meaning for an airplane trip or a *fly* is a winged insect.

13. **School:** is a special building or *school* is a slang term for learning informally.

14. **Dope:** is a term used in the Civil Rights era to describe an illegal drug or *dope* is an anachronistic and unacceptable term (shown in some dictionaries) for "a 'stupid' person."

15. **Period:** is a tool used to end a sentence or a *period* is a length of time.

LESSON 5 - SYNONYMS

Here are 10 SYNONYMS. These are words that do not spell the same. They do not sound the same. BUT, they mean the same. This is especially important in reading comprehension and listening skill development. They help in writing skills because you do not need to be redundant or use the same words over and over in essays. Match their meanings of sameness to you.   Then add your ten using this pattern. You may use the dictionary.

1.	diversity _e_	a. useful
2.	bigotry __g_	b. accolades
3.	wisdom _d__	c. helpless
4.	futile _c__	d. sagacity
5.	tributes __b_	e. plural
6.	stipulated _i_	f. believe
7.	viable _a__	g. racism
8.	compel _j__	h. free
9.	assume __f_	i. named
10.	emancipate_h_	j. drive

Add 10 new synonyms here.   (ANSWERS WILL VARY)

1. _________________________   _________________

2. _________________________   _________________

3. _________________________   _________________

4. _________________________   _________________

5. _________________________   _________________

6. _________________________   _________________

7. _________________________   _________________

8. _________________________   _________________

9. _________________________   _________________

10. _________________________   _________________

LESSON 6 - ANTONYMS, VOCABULARY

Here are 10 ANTONYMS: These are words that DO NOT spell the same. They DO NOT sound the same. AND they are directly opposite in meaning. This is especially important in reading comprehension and listening skill development. First, we will teach you. Then you add five more sets to the list in the spaces provided to show us you understand.

Example: Integration   Segregation

1. Peace   Conflict
2. Strong   Weak
3. Abroad   Local
4. Restrained   boundary
5. Jubilant   sad
6. Equitable   Unfair
7. Unity   Division
8. Order   Chaos
9. Sagacity   Ignorance
10. Poverty   Wealth

1____

2____

3____

4____

5____

Match these antonyms using the correct number.

11. Peace _j__   a. Abroad
12. Strong _e__   b. Jubilant
13. Local __a_   c. Order
14. Restrained _d__   d. Unbound
15. Sad _b__   e. Weak
16. Equitable _f__   f. Unfair
17. Unity_g__   g. Division
18. Chaos _c__   h. Wealth
19. Sagacity_i__   i. Ignorance
20. Poverty _h__   j. Conflict

LESSON 7 - MORE ANTONYMS

Here are 10 ANTONYMS: These are words that DO NOT spell the same. They DO NOT sound the same. AND they are DIRECTLY OPPOSITE in meaning. This is especially important in reading comprehension and listening skill development. First, we will teach you. Then you add five more sets to the list in the spaces provided to show us you understand. Finally, match the meanings.

1.	Amicable	Unfriendly
2.	Introvert	Outgoing
3.	Weak	Powerful
4.	Tenacity	Loose
5.	Inform	Withhold
6.	Certain	Inevitable
7.	Purposeful	Intentional
8.	Divide	Add
9.	Contribute	Separate
10.	Unafraid	Valor

Now write five additional pairs of ANTONYMS.

1. _________________________ / _________________________
2. _________________________ / _________________________
3. _________________________ / _________________________
4. _________________________ / _________________________
5. _________________________ / _________________________

Match these ANTONYMS:

1.	Introvert	_10_	intentional
2.	Weak	_1_	outgoing
3.	Amicable	_4_	valor
4.	afraid	_6_	loose
5.	Certain	_2_	powerful
6.	Tenacity	_5_	inevitable
7.	Inform	_9_	separate
8.	divide	_3_	unfriendly
9.	contribute	_7_	tell
10.	purposeful	_8_	add

LESSON 8 - SPELLING

CHALLENGE YOUR FRIENDS! Here is a list of 15 words that are not all spelled correctly. One is correct on each line. Circle the correct one. This is especially important in writing, spelling, reading comprehension, and other literacy skill development. Add five more n*ew and difficult* words from the lessons in CHOSEN VESSELS (or any American history lessons) in the spaces provided. Discuss them with your leader.

1. **American**	Amercan	Americin	Americain
2. Patreot	**Patriot**	Patriok	Patroit
3. Unittedd	Uniteed	**United**	Unnnitted
4. **Civil**	Civel	Civvel	Civiel
5. Constiituion	Cunstition	**Constitution**	Constiution
6. Ancesstors	**Ancestors**	Anacestos	Anscetors
7. **Continent**	Countint	conttinet	Cuntinnent
8. Plege	pleadge	**pledge**	Pleagge
9. Histry	Histroy	**History**	Histrory
10. **Enforcement**	Enforcment	Enforment	Enforsement
11. Weallth	Waleth	Wealeth	**Wealth**
12. **Faith**	Fiath	Fathe	Faetjh
13. **Allegiance**	Alegiance	Aledgiance	A lligiyunce
14. Centruy	Cintry	**Century**	Cenntury
15. Idigenous	Indegous	**Indigenous**	Idianeous

LESSON 10 - PHONICS, SPELLING, LISTENING, SPEAKING

Here are 20 words that are spelled correctly. Write the last sound you make when you say each of these words. This is especially important in writing, spelling, phonics, and speaking. Discuss these with your leader or classmates.

1. Hope — 1
2. Rights — 1
3. Citizen — 3
4. Revolution — 4
5. Emancipation — 5
6. Slavery — 3
7. Brutality — 4
8. Nation — 2
9. United States — 3   1
10. Semiquincentennial — 7
11. Racism — 3
12. Liberty — 3
13. Indigenous — 4
14. Christianity — 5
15. American — 4
16. Reconstruction — 4
17. E Pluribus unum — 1   3   2
18. Massacres — 3
19. Abolitionist — 5
20. Supremacy — 4

BONUS

21. Inequality — 5
22. Christianity — 5
23. Auctions — 2

1. _______________ ____
2. _______________ ____
3. _______________ ____
4. _______________ ____
5. _______________ ____

LESSON 12 - SEQUENCE, RECALL, MEMORIZATION

Arrange these documents in chronological order of preparedness for the Semiquincentennial. Write a number from 1- 9 to show their order of occurrences in our history. (Ask your leader if you might review your lesson ____ in your "CHOSEN VESSELS" book. The chapter will help you to recall this information and the order of occurrences. Write a brief explanation for how it helped Americans in our diverse culture.

Order of Issuance   Designed to Help Americans

Year: _____1787_________ **The United States Constitution**: ______(1)_______outlines the framework of the federal government and protects individual rights and liberties.

Year: ____1863__________ **The Emancipation**: ______(2)________It declared all slaves in the Southern territories or confederate states free if they joined the Union.

Year: _______1868____ The **14th Amendment**: _____(5)______ granted full citizenship under the law to those who were formally enslaved. ________________________________

Year: _______1865_____ **The 13th Amendment**: _________ (3) ____________abolished slavery in the United States____

Year: ________1870____ **The 15th Amendment**: __________ (6)__________granted Black American men the right to vote.

Year: _____1964____ **The Civil Rights Act of 1964**: __________(8)___________President Lyndon B. JOHNSON signed into law the prohibiting of discrimination based on race, color, religion, sex, or national origin.

Year____1948_________ **Executive order 1981**: ________(7)___________mandated the racial integration of the US Armed Services.

Year___ 1965 ______ **The Voting Rights Act of 1965**: ______(9)______Law signed by President Johnson aimed at overcoming legal barriers, at the state and local levels which prevented African Americans from exercising the right to vote._________________________

Year___1866___________ **The Civil Rights Act of 1866**: ____(4)______Act was passed to grant full citizenship and guarantee the rights of the freed slaves. ________________________

LESSON 13 - READING COMPREHENSION, SUPPORTING DETAILS, WRITING

Arrange these eras of movements leading up to the Semiquincentennial. Write a number from 1- 6 to show their level of chronological order. Write a brief explanation for how you think it helped Americans in our diverse culture to become more united. Be prepared to defend your choices.

1__________3__________ **Jim Crow** __________________________________

____

____

2__________2__________ **Reconstruction** __________________________

____

____

3__________1__________ **Slavery** __________________________________

____

____

4__________5__________ **Black Lives Matter** ______________________

____

____

5__________6__________ **Sesquincentennial** ________________________

____

____

BONUS

6__________4__________ **Civil Rights Movement** __________________

____

____

LESSON 14 - TRUE OR FALSE: FOR DISCUSSION

These statements are true or False. Write T or F on the lines provided after the number. These lessons help with the memorization of historical facts and data, research, reading comprehension, and critical thinking skills.

1. __T__ White Americans helped organize the National Association for the Advancement of Colored People (NAACP). The NAACP was established in 1909 in New York by a group of Black and White Americans. Mary White Ovington, Henry Moskowitz, and William English Walling were wealthy, academic, and patriotic Americans who wanted to help America to rid its hatred and racist views of Black Americans.

2. __T__ African Americans or Black-skinned people were living in America before Columbus "discovered" it or slaves were sold on its shores. Many historians share the fact that Blacks were here long before Columbus. The Indigenous people report that "they came in boats and traded with gold-tipped spears", writings, and mathematics, were not uncommon.

3. __T__ The "Lift Every Voice and Sing" lyrics are older than the" Star-Spangled Banner" lyrics.

4. __T__ Many White American slave owners were the recipients of reparations for having to free their slaves before blacks ever conceived of the idea.

5. __T__ A small number of Blacks Americans and Indians owned slaves and fought against the abolition or ending this evil and brutal system in America.

6. __T__ The 19th Amendment extended the right to vote to White women in 1920, but it did not extend this same "equal right" to vote to Black Women at that time.

7. __F__ Only White Americans fought in the American military branches of the United States of America. Black Americans fought in every War even in colonial times.

8. __T__ Even though the squalid conditions did not break their spirit, and no one was ever held accountable for the Leesburg Stockade in Georgia, three of the 15 girls may still celebrate the Semiquincentennial in person.

9. __F__ Nat Turners Rebellion and John Browns's Raid at Harper's Ferry was a success.

10. __F__ All major fights against racism and division in our diverse communities have been done by Black Americans.

BONUS

11. __T__ America's diversity is increasing by the minute. Immigration in Texas, Arizona, New Mexico has shown new immigrant numbers.

LESSON 15 - READING VOCABULARY AND COMPREHENSION

Scholars will acquire and extend their academic vocabulary in order to be successful in college. Here are 10 sample words on that level. Read the list and their meanings. Then place the correct word in the sentences below. This helps your literacy skills in all areas. It helps you to speak, listen, and read on a college level.

1. **Discredit:** put to shame; disgrace.
2. **Emulate:** try to equal or imitate.
3. **Integrity:** morally upright, honesty, sincerity
4. **Opponents:** opposite sides,
5. **Enhance:** add to something; give more
6. **Inevitable:** bound to happen
7. **Resilient:** bounce back after loss, return
8. **Exasperated:** irritated greatly, infuriated, made very angry
9. **Exemplary:** commendable, exceptional
10. **Inconsequential:** Trivial, doesn't matter, not leading to consequences

Place these words in these sentences. Skip the ones that you do not know and come back to them.

1. Our favorite, smart and _______**9**_______ candidate was behind as the polls were drawing to a close.

2. Of course, we were frustrated, _______**8**_______, and disappointed at the voters' turnout and polls.

3. The _______**4**_______, or our competition, had an outstanding campaign leader.

4. The weather did not help or _______**5**_______ our chances and possibilities either.

5. We will _______**2**_______ and imitate some of their speeches and strategies during the next election.

6. We cannot _______**1**_______ their efforts by accusing them of cheating.

7. Losing a tough race like this is not _______**10**_______, and the evaluations of each department's manager will be rigorous.

8. However, if we keep working this hard, it is _______**6**_______ that our candidate will win in a run-off.

9. Our candidate shows _______**3**_____ on and off the campaign trail.

10. A little rest and relaxation will help him to bounce back and become even more _______**7**_______ during the next term.

LESSON 16 - VOCABULARY, READING COMPREHENSION, WRITING, SPELLING

Match these college-level readiness words and their meanings. You may use a dictionary. Then write a sentence in the spaces below using the word. This will help to increase your college-level readiness vocabulary. It helps to familiarize you with the many literacy tools available in your personal dictionary and hand-held devices. Discuss any concerns.

Part A: Vocabulary

1.   Sagacity ___f__
2.   Tenacious __h__
3.   Transient __e___
4.   Vindicate __i__
5.   Tactful __g___
6.   Wary __b__
7.   Subtle __d__
8.   Submissive __a__
9.   Substantiate __c__
10. Extrovert __k__

Part B: Meanings

a. meek and humble

b. watchful, alert

c. verify, confirm,

d. elusive, sly

e. not stable, moving, in motion

f. wisdom, knowing, wise

g. polite, diplomatic

h. hangs on, unmovable

i. clear from blame or wrongdoings

j. outgoing

Choose any 5 new words and write five sentences here. (Answers will vary)

1.   ____
____

2.   ____
____

3.   ____
____

4.   ____
____

5.   ____
____

LESSON 17 - READING FOR UNDERSTANDING

Some amazing and amusing historical data notes from the contents of CHOSEN VESSELS are included here. Understanding what you read is a lifetime investment. Place the proper words (synonyms, antonyms, etc.) in the sentences to help them to make sense to you.

1. The ___**d**___ of the gold broke the axle on the wagon's back wheels.
   a. Sneak   b. steal   c. wait   d. weight   e. team

2. Our earliest ancestors first church services, praise and ___**d**___ were not held in sanctuaries. They were held in isolated, secretive spots called 'hush harbors'.
   a. Base   b. steps   c. towns   d. worship   e. dogs

3. If you are queried, or you are ___**b**___ about the number of soap bubbles that are in a bar of soap, would you be concerned about the motive?
   a. answered   b. questioned   c. written   d. told   e. kept

4. An American history course to show the uniting of our states should be ___**c**___ for every US citizen in our diverse society.
   a. vaccine   b. unity   c. mandatory   d. hidden   e. used

5. At least ___**c**___ Indigenous tribes were represented during the formation of the US Constitution council meetings.
   a. further   b. colony   c. eight   d. better   e. ate

6. You do not have to drive ___**b**___ to vote in most elections.
   a. pen   b. far   c. for   d. little   e. book

7. If the Constitution is filled with racism and ___**a**___, it cannot serve a diverse population.
   a. bigotry   b. single   c. outgoing   d. light   e. unused

8. Cotton, corn, and sugar cane were hot ___**c**___ in making America a wealthy nation.
   a. Homes   b. roads   c. commodities   d. rode   e. cars

9. Some World War II ammunition was made from ___**a**___ plastics and other materials.
   a. Recycled   b. powerless   c. motion   d. weather   e. crops

10. If it transpires before the Semiquincentennial, it will ___**e**___ before 2026.
    a. Win   b. vote   c. false   d. law   e. happen

LESSON 18 - SPELLING, PHONICS

Scholars do not fear using words that are not a part of their everyday conversations. They can break them down into smaller parts to gain meaning and the proper way of pronouncing them, phonetically. With the aid of your English dictionary's pronunciation symbols, you can unlock the key to speaking or saying any word. Practice these 10 words and break them into each part you hear. Read. Spell these words without looking at them. Use your dictionary if you are unsure of the meaning.

FOR PRACTICE IN KNOWING HOW TO MAKE THE CORRECT PRONUNCIATIONS WHEN ENCOUNTERING BIG WORDS IN THE FUTURE. COPY EVERY MARK OR SYMBOL USED IN YOUR PRONUNCIATION KEY FOR EACH WORD LISTED. *(DICTIONARY KEYS WILL VARY)*

1. Monolithic
2. Humongous
3. Divisiveness
4. Anachronistic
5. Sagacity
6. Constitution
7. Bibliotherapy
8. Semiquincentennial
9. Capitalism
10. E Pluribus unum

a. ______ ____ ____ ____
b. _____ ____ ____
c. _____ ____ ____ ____
d. _____ ____ ____ ____ ____ ___
e. _____ ____ ____ ____
f. ____ ____ ____ ____
g. ___ ___ ____ ___ ___ ___
h. ___ ___ ____ ___ ___ ___ ___
i. ____ ____ ____ ___ ___
j. ____ ____ ___ ___ ___ __

MATCH THESE MEANINGS. USE YOUR DICTIONARY FOR MORE UNDERSTANDING.

11. Monolithic _j_
12. Humongous _a_
13. Divisiveness _h_
14. Anachronistic _b_
15. Sagacity _i_
16. Constitution _c_
17. Bibliotherapy f_
18. Semiquincentennial _e_
19. Capitalism _d_
20. E Pluribus unum _g_

a. huge, gigantic, very large ___
b. old-fashioned, out-of-date
c. basic beliefs, rights, laws established
d. an economic system
e. a celebratory period for 250 years
f. using books to treat mental stress
g. out of many, one
h. separate, individualistic, segregate
i. wisdom, knowledge, wise
j. one sided view, opinionated

ABOUT THE AUTHOR

Elizabeth Grady Branch, EdD

Elizabeth Grady Branch, EdD is a proud mother, grandmother, educator, and faith-based author. Born into abject poverty in deep East Texas, she graduated from the segregated Fred Douglass High School in Jacksonville. She received a bachelor's degree in Elementary Education, from Jarvis Christian College (now University), a Master's degree from Texas Southern University, and a Doctorate in Education from North Texas State University (now University of North Texas). Her job and career experiences spanned the gamut. Standouts included migrant cotton picker, waitressing, seasonal field worker, and other menial jobs to help the family's income. Her career after college included the joys and rewards of becoming a K-College-level teacher, administrator, and small business owner. Having been blessed with such a wide range of successful experiences, plus living and thriving thru the part of American history known as "Jim Crow" and the Civil Rights Movement, makes her a highly qualified contender to promote this agenda. It is designed to instill pride, faith, personal nobility, love, and hope in the youth of color in America. Her curriculum materials and old-school wisdom gained from her past are applicable today. Dr. Branch is the author of "Intercepting Tendencies of Violent Behavior in Inner City Youth" published by the Global Publishing company. She is a co-author of "Reading Academic Skills for Culturally Diverse Students" published by Simon and Schuster, "Scrambling to Master Basic English Sentence Structure" by CT Publishing Company, and "Choosing to Lift Every Voice and Sing" published by Xlibris.

ABOUT THE EDITORS

JOKWON BAGBY, MS

Jokwon James Bagby was born in Ft. Worth, Texas. He attended schools in the Dallas/Ft. Worth area, including the Prime Prep Academy in Dallas under Coach Dion Sander's leadership and efforts. Bagby speaks highly of the enriching experiences he received while there. He graduated from Timberview High School in Arlington and enrolled in Texas State University in San Marcos. He received a Bachelor's and a Master's in Spanish while attending school there. He loves teaching and has taught at various levels of academia since graduating. Due to his love for teaching the language and fluency skills demonstrated amongst his peers, he was immediately hired into the teaching field at the college level. He became an adjunct professor at the University of North Texas and Dallas County. Bagby is the author of the book, "Successful Elements," which emphasizes the importance of personal growth and how it can impact future generations. A combination of these teaching skills and other academic experiences helped to make valuable contributions to the information included in this workbook.

JAMESE MICHELLE BRANCH

Jamese M. Branch was born in Ft. Worth, Texas. She is a high school graduate of the Fort Worth Academy of Fine Arts. She attended college at Southern Methodist University in Dallas and graduated from the University of Texas at Austin, Texas. Her degree is in Radio-Television- Film. She is presently employed at the Fort Worth Report as the Marketing and Events Manager, a local digital news outlet that covers community development topics and concerns. Jamese is proud to engage in writing and conversing with young adults from various backgrounds about pressing diversity and inclusion issues. She looks for the opportunity to make a difference using her natural and academic skills and talents.

YVONNE ROSE

Yvonne Rose, a native of Boston/Dorchester, Massachusetts, is the **Associate Publisher and Senior Editor** at Amber Communications Group, Inc. Ms. Rose began her stint at Amber Books in 1998 as the co-author of the Company's flagship title, the national bestseller, *Is Modeling for You? The Handbook and Guide for the Young Aspiring Black Model.* (Amber Books)

Since 2004, when Yvonne was appointed Director of Quality Press for Self-Published authors, she has *ghost-written, co-written and edited* hundreds of top selling non-fiction titles, including: *Rising up from the Blood*: *A Legacy Reclaimed—A Bridge Forward The Autobiography of Sarah Washington O'Neal Rush, The Great-Granddaughter of Booker T. Washington* (Solid Rock Books) by Sarah Washington O'Neal Rush; *Fighting for Your Life: The African American Criminal Justice Survival Guide* (Amber Books) by John Elmore, Esq.; *Led by the Spirit: A Sharecropper's Son Tells His Story of Love, Happiness, Success and Survival* (Strickland Books) by Robuster Strickland; *Let Them Play...The Story of the MGAA* (MGAA Books) by John David; *The Messman: A World War II Hero Tells His Story of Survival and Segregation on the Battleship North Carolina* (Quality Books) by Yvonne Rose and John Seagraves; and *People to Know in Black History & Beyond (Volumes 1, 2 and 3)* (Bob Lee Enterprises) by Doctor Bob Lee.

PROJECT STAND-UP is a 501 (c)(3) non-profit organization previously operating under the umbrella of Man in the Mirror, a community-based organization. PROJECT STAND-UP began with a focus on youth within Tarrant County. Recently, PROJECT STAND-UP has renewed its commitment to serving low-income, disadvantaged, and displaced youth AND adults beyond county lines. Our mission is the pursuit of the following principles:

- *Commitment*: To instill and inspire pro-social, civil behaviors, friendships, entrepreneurial and strong interpersonal skills, and a sense of hope for the future.

- *Responsibility*: To empower individuals in establishing higher educational standards, career goals, and rising above poverty levels.

- *Possibility*: To expand the perspective of individuals and families to make them aware of life's possibilities.

- *Support*: To recognize, energize, influence, and/or provide for people in a caring, inclusive learning environment.

FOR FURTHER INFORMATION, VISIT
WWW.PROJECT STAND-UP.ORG
OR EMAIL: THEPROJECTSTANDUP@GMAIL.COM

www.ingramcontent.com/pod-product-compliance
Lightning Source LLC
Chambersburg PA
CBHW051633170726
48000CB00025B/3053